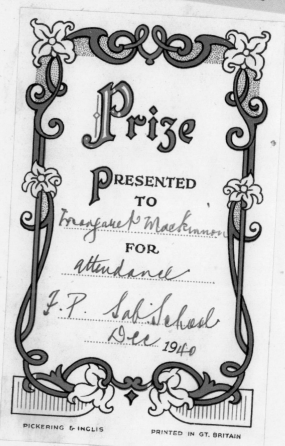

Prize

Presented
TO

Margaret Mackinnon

FOR

attendance

F.P. Sab. School
Dec 1940

PICKERING & INGLIS   PRINTED IN GT. BRITAIN

JOAN HORNS BURNT TO DEATH AT SMITHFIELD, LONDON
(Chapter V)

"They loved not their lives unto death."

TWELVE YOUTHFUL MARTYRS

WHO LAID DOWN THEIR LIVES
FOR THE MASTER'S SAKE

BY

ESTHER E. ENOCK

Author of "Twelve Marvellous Men,"
"Twelve Mighty Missionaries," "The
Quest of Three," etc., etc.   ::

LONDON:

PICKERING & INGLIS Ltd.

14 PATERNOSTER ROW, E.C.4

and at Glasgow, Edinburgh, Manchester, Liverpool

LONDON	-	- 14 PATERNOSTER ROW, E.C.4
GLASGOW	-	- 229 BOTHWELL STREET, C.2
MANCHESTER		- 135 DEANSGATE, 3
LIVERPOOL		- 5 HOPE WAY, 8
EDINBURGH		- 29 GEORGE IV BRIDGE, 1
NEW YORK		- LOIZEAUX BROS., 19 WEST 21ST ST.
TORONTO	-	- HOME EVANGEL, 418 CHURCH ST., 2

TWELVE NOBLE LIVES

Titles as follows

1.	Twelve Marvellous Men,	Esther E. Enock
2.	Twelve Mighty Missionaries,	Esther E. Enock
3.	Twelve Wonderful Women,	E. H. Farrance
4.	Twelve Brave Boys,	Esther E. Enock
5.	Twelve Famous Evangelists,	James Stephen
6.	Twelve Clever Girls,	J. A. W. Hamilton
7.	Twelve Youthful Martyrs,	Esther E. Enock

Made and Printed in Great Britain   17389

Contents

Illustrations

TWELVE
YOUTHFUL MARTYRS

CHAPTER I

Thomas Drowry

THE BLIND BOY WHO COULD SEE

IT was February, in the year 1555. The small but old city of Gloucester was bathed in the bright sunshine which we sometimes get in that early month; and snowdrops and violets were peeping forth, no doubt then, as they do now.

Birds, chirruping in trees and hedges, were beginning to think where they would build their nests, and here and there the palm willow (catkins, as we call it) could be seen. All around one could see the promise of spring. Not all the sorrow and persecution which went on at this time under the cruel rule of Queen Mary could alter that—spring still came with its resurrection lessons and joys.

There was a great stir in the city of Gloucester. People were going forth of it in crowds, to see something, or some one.

In a dark and dreary dungeon in this same city a boy was sitting. His name was THOMAS DROWRY, and he was about 15 years of age, and had been thrown into prison because he refused to turn Roman Catholic. He sits there in that dreary place, spring in his heart, thinking thoughts which cheer and brighten. He cannot see the reeking walls of his prison, nor the unpleasantness of his surroundings, for he is quite blind.

But his spiritual eyes are looking upon such glories that the things of earth have vanished for the present. He has been enabled to look upward to Heaven where all is joy and peace, and where the wicked can trouble no more. He proved the truth of those words: "Our light affliction, which is but for a moment, worketh for us a far more exceeding and eternal weight of glory; while we look not at the things which are seen, but at the things which are not seen; for the things which are seen are temporal; but the things which are not seen are eternal" (2 Cor. 4. 17, 18)—and his spiritual eyes were gazing steadfastly at those eternal things.

A key grated in the ponderous lock of his dungeon door, and the jailer entered. "Ha! boy, I've come to release thee, but unless that tongue of thine refrains from its unwisdom, I shall soon be having thee under lock and key again."

"So be it, for I will not deny my Lord, God helping me," answered the boy with a smile, as he rose to his feet with difficulty.

The man looked at him in surprise. This hardihood in one so young, so afflicted, amazed him, and sometimes he wondered whence the courage and endurance came.

Out in the open and the sweet fresh air, THOMAS DROWRY found one waiting for him with news. Bishop HOOPER was on his way to Gloucester City, condemned to be burnt there. All along the road for a mile outside the walls, people had gone to meet him, and cheer his progress, for he was much beloved.

THOMAS DROWRY soon found himself

among the great concourse of those which
had gathered to welcome that devoted
man who, in two days' time, was to suffer
martyrdom. This was February 7th, 1555.

"I must see him to-morrow," Thomas
Drowry said to his companion. "Where
lodgeth he? Dost know?" "At Ingram's
house. But there will be guards who will
not permit thee to have speech with him.
Moreover, to be friends with the bishop is
to incur the displeasure of his judges."

"Nevertheless, I must try," replied the
blind boy; and there was no indecision in
his tones.

Next day, according to his resolve, he
groped his way to the house, and, "after
long intercession made to the guard, ob-
obtained licence to speak with Master
Hooper." The meeting was a comfort to
both. The condemned man spoke to
Thomas of the faith which sustained them,
and when he had asked him the cause of his
imprisonment, bade him be of good courage, and be strengthened in that faith.

Looking steadfastly upon the blind boy,
who, though he could not see him, was

conscious of his gaze, and even of the tears which stood in his eyes, the bishop said: "Ah, poor boy! God hath taken from thee thy natural sight, for what reason He best knoweth, but He hath given thee another sight more precious, for He hath endued thy soul with the eye of knowledge and of faith. "

Thomas Drowry told him that this was indeed the case, and that he had been enabled in his dark dungeon to see something of the bliss and joy they would have in the presence of their Lord. And the man who was to suffer long and cruel torture in the flames on the morrow (his was the longest and most cruel torturings of those who were burnt) felt his own courage and faith increased by the simple confession.

And so they parted, not to exchange any words again on earth, but we may be sure that in the Heavenly Home—all rough and stormy days passed—they would tell each other much.

Thomas Drowry was soon thrown into prison again, where he waited long weeks

the pleasure of the Chancellor, Dr.
Williams, to summon him to trial. Dr.
Williams was not quite a stranger to
Thomas. The boy had often heard him
preach, for the Chancellor was in office
during the reign of Edward VI at "the
Cathedral of Gloucester."

In the consistory then of this church,
Thomas Drowry was at last brought before
Dr. Williams, and Thomas Taylor, the
Registrar.

Dr. Williams put the usual question:
"Dost thou believe that after the words of
consecration spoken by the priest, there
remaineth *the very real body of Christ*
in the sacrament of the altar?"

Thomas Drowry knew that the bread is
taken only in *remembrance* of the Lord's
death—that it remained *bread*, and was
not a thing to be worshipped, and he said
so.

Dr. Williams asked him who had taught
him that. "You, Master Chancellor. You
preached there"—turning in the direction
of the pulpit—"you said that the sacrament
was to be received spiritually by faith,

and not carnally as the Papists have heretofore taught. "

This was awkward for the Chancellor. It showed so clearly that for convenience' sake he could preach one thing in Edward's reign (Thomas had named the day of the sermon) and another in Queen Mary's.

He looked angrily for a moment at the daring boy, then said: "Well, do as I have done and thou shalt live as I do, and escape burning. "

"Though you can dispense yourself, and mock with God and your conscience, yet will I not so do, " Thomas answered.

The enraged and convicted Chancellor then read the sentence of condemnation against the boy, in spite of the Registrar's protest that someone else should do it. Thomas Drowry was taken back to his dungeon till May 5th, when he was led to the place of execution in Gloucester, with a bricklayer, Thomas Croker, "condemned also for the like testimony of the truth, where, both together in one fire, they most constantly and joyfully yielded their souls into the hands of the Lord Jesus."

After that fire Thomas Drowry's eyes were opened on the glories of Heaven indeed! He found, as he had believed, that "the sufferings of this present time are not worthy to be compared with the glory which shall be revealed in us. "

Chapter II

Willie Hunter

THE BRENTWOOD MARTYR

I FANCY I see a boy standing in his quiet room—on the table near the window is a *Book*. He lays his hand upon it irresolutely, then turns abruptly away. Why waste the sunny hour reading the Bible? And so he goes downstairs heedless of that Treasure, for the possession and reading of which, many have yielded up themselves to cruel torture and even death itself. All honour to their names.

Now I see another boy. His name is WILLIAM HUNTER. He is dressed as boys were in the days of Queen Mary, and is walking along the road to Weald, a town near Brentwood, Essex. There he enters a church. No service is going on at the time, and he goes quietly up to the big Bible chained there. Unlike the first boy we saw, William has no Bible of his own, but he loves the Book, and pores over it for a long time, then goes home refreshed by reading of his Saviour and his Heavenly home.

William Hunter was born about 1536, during the reign of Henry VIII, and at the time of this story was nearly 19 years of age.

He was a clever boy; his parents had brought him up well, sending him to school, teaching him to love the Bible, and to do as it says. He went to London when he left school to be apprenticed to a silk-weaver, THOMAS TAYLOR. This was in 1553. Queen Mary had just come to the throne, and at her behest priests were compelling people to worship the bread at mass, which bread the priests declared was by their consecration turned into the very body of Christ. William Hunter, and others like-minded knew that it remained bread, and that to worship it was idolatry.

So when Easter Sunday came William refused to go to Mass, and was told that he would be brought before Bonner, the Bishop of London. This threat so terrified Thomas Taylor, William's master, that he sent William straight down to his home in Brentwood, "lest he should come in danger himself through having him in his house."

At Brentwood, as we have seen, he had some happy times, studying the chained Bible in the Weald chapel. But this was not for long. A man named Atwell, whose duty was to point out heretics, found him reading it one day, and as he could not prevail against William in discussion fell into a great rage. "You shall broil for this!" said he, and went to find the vicar, and to tell him of William's wickedness in reading the Bible.

The vicar was quite near—"in the ale-house over against the chapel"—and rushed in to William, and accused him of being a heretic. The outcome of it was that William, in order to save his parents trouble hid himself, but when he heard that the priest had threatened to imprison his father if he did find the son, gave himself up, and was put into the stocks.

Next day the constable brought him

2

before Master Brown (later made a knight by Queen Mary), and Master Brown became so infuriated by the lad's quiet constancy and simple faith in the Saviour that he "left off talk," and "made a letter," and sent William with the constable, to Bonner in London.

Bonner tried to make him recant—to deny all he had said before—but William said: "I will *not* recant, by God's help." Then said Bonner: "Thou art ashamed to bear a faggot (the public way of showing recantation), but speak the word here and now, between me and thee, and I promise thee it shall go no further, and thou shalt go home again without any hurt." Again said William firmly: "I will not. No, never, while I live; God willing."

He had two days and two nights in the stocks, then the Bishop saw him again, and ordered him to prison with heavy chains. He asked William his age. William told him, "Nineteen." "Well," said the Bishop, "you will be burned ere you be twenty years old, if you will not yield yourself better than you have done yet."

The Bishop allowed him a halfpenny a day for food or drink. For nine months this brave boy lay in prison—going four times before the Bishop, but William turned no whit from his steadfastness. Finally he was condemned to be burnt, and was thrown into Newgate prison till he could be taken to Brentwood and be burnt there.

William wrote to his mother saying that he himself was in as good health and prosperity as ever he had been. He asked her prayers, and his brother Robert's for himself, in this his prosperous journey which he was going, to obtain a crown of everlasting life. And then he came to Brentwood, and stayed at the Swan Inn there, where he had opportunity of exhorting many of his friends to be faithful, and to suffer death rather than disown the Saviour by the idolatry of the Mass.

So passed Saturday, Sunday, Monday. On Tuesday, March 26th, 1555, the sheriff master Brocket, hastened to set forward the burning.

The sheriff's son came into the parlour

of the inn where William sat waiting, and said to him, as he put an arm through his: "Be not afraid of these men which are here present with bows, bills, and weapons, ready, prepared to bring you to the place where you shall be burned."

And William replied to this brave and loving boy: "I thank God I am not afraid; for I have cast my count what it will cost me already." And the boy could say no more for weeping.

Then they left the Inn, and walked to the place where all the people had assembled to see William burnt. His parents were there. "God be with you," he said. "We shall meet again, when we shall be merry."

He walked to the stake, and Richard Ponde, the bailiff, chained him to it. Standing there, William cried: "Son of God, shine on me!" Immediately a beam of sunshine pierced the dark clouds, and fell upon him so brilliantly that he was obliged to look another way; "whereat the people mused, for it was so dark a little while before."

William's brother, Robert, was asked by the priest to give William a popish book that he might recant, but Robert would not touch it.

"I am not afraid, " William said. Then lifting his hands he cried: "Lord! Lord! receive my spirit!" His head went down into the smothering smoke, and thus he went away on his prosperous journey to Heaven.

CHAPTER III

Agnes Prest

THE EXETER MARTYR

ALONG picturesque Magdalene Road, Exeter, on January 10th, 1531, a crowd of people was moving towards Heavitree. At Livery Dole a stake had been set up, and there Thomas Benet was burnt to death for refusing to worship the Virgin and the wafer which the priests declared to be the real body of Christ. Among the throng surrounding the noble martyr was a woman, on a visit to Exeter —AGNES PREST by name

After witnessing the brave and patient endurance of Thomas Benet she was a changed being. From that time she attended secret Protestant meetings, "preachings," in the Mint, off Fore Street, Exeter, where she learnt so quickly of the Scriptures that she was able to give chapter and verse of any text she heard.

Her husband was an ardent Roman Catholic, and on her return home to Trewan, Launceston, he constantly troubled her because she would not go to Mass, or worship the wafer. Her children, too, were very unkind to her. At last her husband told the priest of her "obstinacy," and Agnes's persecution began in earnest.

Flitte, the priest, called and questioned her, and soon after his departure she fled, and took refuge with some friends, supporting herself by carding wool, a work at which she was very clever, and teaching salvation through Christ alone, to any she met. Thus it was not for long that she could remain hidden; she was taken prisoner, conveyed to Exeter, and brought before the bishop, Turberville (or Tuberville).

"Foolish woman," said he, "thou hast spoken against the most blessed sacrament of the altar, the body of Christ. If it be as I am informed, thou art worthy to be burned;" and much more in the same strain.

"Sikerly, sir," Agnes answered, "I

would rather die than do any worship to
that idol which, with your mass, you
make a god. *Let it be your god; it shall not
be mine*: for my Saviour sitteth on the
right hand of God, and doth pray for me."

Her courage, and her brave replies to
his many questions, at length so wearied
and enraged the bishop that he would at
once have condemned her, but the chancellor persuaded him to give her a month
in which to recant. She was sent to stay
with the keeper of the prison, with freedom
to come and go about the city. This prison
was in the grounds of the bishop's palace,
not far from the south gate, which was
also used as a prison.

Even in charge of the keeper she seemed
without fear, telling the friars who visited
her that they misguided souls when they
taught people to worship a false god of
their own making—a piece of bread: that
they sold their prayers for money—they
made people buy pardons—they taught
people that they should pray upon beads—
should pray to the saints—"and a thousand
more abominations. And yet you say you

come for my profit, and to save my soul. No! No!! *Christ hath saved me.* Farewell ye, with your salvation."

During this month she visited St. Peter's Church (the Cathedral) and spoke on idolatry there to a Dutchman engaged in repairing the noses of some images of saints which had been destroyed in the reign of Edward VI. He denounced her, and she was put into a dungeon of the prison, and had no more liberty. Whilst in this dungeon she had several visitors. One was Daniel, a man who had been a great preacher of the Gospel in the reign of Edward. He came to persuade her to recant, by which she perceived that he had turned from the simple Gospel for fear of man. Agnes Prest, instead of being persuaded by him to forsake her Lord, exhorted him to repent, as Peter did, and, like Peter, he would be forgiven and restored.

Another visitor was the wife of a man named Walter Ralegh, a sweet and good woman, who, too, tried to persuade Agnes to recant. Agnes showed her the wickedness and idolatry of the mass, and spoke so clearly on the Scriptures, quoting them so truly that Dame Ralegh on her return to her husband, said: "That if God were not with her (Agnes) she could not speak such things, the which I was not able to answer her, who can read, and she cannot."

Two dear Protestant brothers, William and John Kede, visited her, too, and much comfort did she receive from them, whilst much did she strengthen them.

Then, at a day she was hailed to the Guildhall, before the bishop and the mayor, John Petre, and she faced her judges bravely, refusing to acknowledge their "bready god," and telling them a few plain Gospel truths which showed the falsity and wickedness of the Romish Church. She was then, "by the secular arm," condemned to be burnt for heresy.

They took her back to the bishop's prison, or Lollard's Tower, as it was often called, in the palace grounds just on the City wall. Some of it still remains to this day, including the archway at which she entered. Inside on the right, there are narrow steps up and down. Agnes was conducted to the steps leading down to the dungeons—but they led up, nevertheless—for she was nearing Heaven all the time. She rejoiced to suffer for Him Who loved and had given Himself for her.

On August 15th, 1557, in charge of Sheriff Robert Midwinter, she left the dungeon, and passing out of the City through the South Gate, walked up Southernhay West. It would take about twenty minutes to reach the spot where she was to suffer, which was nearly at the top of the street.

What would her thoughts be as she traversed the road from the prison? Would she think of the crowds gathering around? Would she pray for those who did not know the Saviour? Would she pray for her persecutors? Would she pray for strength to endure as seeing Him Who is invisible, when the stake and faggots came within her view?

Her heroic end showed that strength was given. People had gathered on the walls to see her at the place of burning.

There she was tied to the stake—"as simple a woman to see as any man might behold; of a very little and short stature, somewhat thick, about 54 years of age. She had a cheerful countenance, so lively, as though she had been prepared for that day of her marriage to meet the Lamb. There," says Foxe, "with much patience she took her cruel death, and so ended this mortal life as constant a woman in the faith of Christ as ever was upon the earth."

Her last words, as the people stood by watching the flames spring up round her were: "'I am the Resurrection and the Life,' saith Christ; 'he that believeth in Me, though he were dead, yet shall he live, and he that believeth in Me shall never die'" (John 11. 25, 26). And then her spirit took flight, away from the staring crowd and consuming flame, to be for ever with the Lord.

CHAPTER IV

John Leaf

THE TALLOW CHANDLER'S BOY

IN the year 1536, when King Henry VIII
was reigning in England—the year in
which Anne Boleyn (mother of the great
Queen Elizabeth), was put to death, a little
boy was born at Kirby-Moorside, in the
County of York. His name was JOHN LEAF.
His parents must have been poor people,
for John was never taught to read or write.

It was a troubled England into which
this little boy was born and in which
he was to live but twenty years.

There was rioting in Lincolnshire and
Yorkshire, and when John Leaf was two
years old many of the rioters had been
put to death, though King Henry had
promised them pardon.

But in that same year, 1538, a wonderful
thing was done by this same King Henry—
for God can work His will through good

men or bad men—and this wonderful thing was the placing of the Bible in English, in every church. The King ordered it, so that any who wished to read it could do so. This Bible was the translation made by William Tyndale.

He had been put to death in October, 1536, for that very work, and now, two years after, that very king who had him killed, is setting up that very Bible in every church. The putting of Tyndale's Bible into the churches, and its use among those who could buy a copy for themselves, spread the Gospel very quickly.

Though little John Leaf could not *read*, he could *hear*, and he heard to some purpose. He learned, through God's Word to put his faith and trust entirely in the Lord Jesus as his Saviour, and to have nothing to do with the superstitions and errors of the Romish Church. King Henry had issued a Proclamation that all doctrines which could not be proved by the Scriptures were not to be regarded, though the Romish Church tried to enforce them.

So John Leaf grew up in a time when the

Bible was a great favourite with the people. When he was eleven years old came King Henry's death, and the accession of the boy-king, Edward VI, the sweet and delicate boy who reigned only six years.

It would be during that reign, probably, that John Leaf left his Yorkshire home, and came to London as an apprentice to Humfrey Gawdy, a tallow chandler, in the parish of Christchurch, in London.

The "Prentice lads" were a very lively lot. Very often they would desert their shops at the cry of "Clubs!" from one of their number, to join in a fight in the street, in which they frequently had broken bones as sole reward.

The shops in those days were mostly open to the streets, rather like our fish-shops, and the "prentices" stood in front or beside their wares shouting to the passers-by "What d'ye lack? What d'ye lack?" and making amusing (and often impertinent) remarks to gain customers.

People had no gas or electricity then, and tallow candles were very important things. So we may imagine that John

3

Leaf was not leading an idle life at Master Humfrey Gawdy's—Tallow Chandler. And John himself was a "light," little though he knew it. His light is shining to this day. You can see it, if you will, and you, too, can shine "like a little candle burning in the night."

As long as the young and gentle King Edward was on the throne, I expect Humfrey Gawdy was well pleased with his quietly behaved apprentice, who liked so much to hear the preachers at Paul's Cross, and the readings from the chained Bibles.

But when Edward died, there came Queen Mary, and she forbade such things, making death the penalty to be paid by those who persisted in these liberties of the Protestant faith. Then, I expect, the tallow chandler would soon begin to look upon John Leaf as a dangerous person to employ, unless the lad could be persuaded to turn Roman Catholic. But this John would not do. He remained firm. As time went on, and persecution of Protestants grew more severe, he became noticed, perhaps spoken about to people who would betray him.

The Alderman in charge of that part of London in the year A.D. 1555 (two years after Queen Mary's accession), began to be very diligent in hunting up heretics. Thus it was that John Leaf, still busy with his wares, "on the Friday before Palm Sunday," was taken, and thrown into prison, the Compter, in Bread Street.

There was a very wonderful prisoner there at the same time, Master John Bradford, and these two Johns were able to help and comfort each other greatly. It would probably be about the end of March when John Leaf was taken. In early June he was brought before Bishop Bonner, and the usual questions were asked.

John refused to embrace the idolatrous belief they wanted, and said that no priest had authority to absolve from sin. He knew there is only one way of cleansing for that—"Nothing but the Blood of Jesus."

The bishop told him he must appear again on the following Monday, June 10th, to hear his sentence of condemnation. But if he thought those few days would change John Leaf he was mistaken.

The bishop on that day (June 10th), "notwithstanding all his persuasions, threats, and promises, found him the same man still; so planted upon the sure rock of truth, that no words or deeds of men could remove him."

Among other things the bishop asked him if he had been Master Roger's scholar. This John Rogers had helped Tyndale in the translation of the New Testament in Antwerp, where many Protestants sought refuge. In King Edward's reign he returned to England and became Vicar of St. Sepulchre's, London, and reader at St. Paul's. He was there till after the accession of Queen Mary. He was burnt at the stake on February 4th, 1555.

John Leaf owned that he was one of this brave and good man's scholars, and that he believed all that he taught, and Bishop Hooper and others lately martyred for their testimony of Christ.

Angrily he was dismissed to prison once more. Two papers were sent to him there: one was a recantation, the other the confession of his faith as made before the bishop. He was to choose which of these he would sign.

John had them both read to him. The recantation he refused. When the reading of his confession of faith was finished, as he could not write, "he took a pin, and so pricking his hand sprinkled the blood upon the said bill, telling the reader thereof to show the bishop that he had sealed the said bill with his blood already."

Early in July he was led to the stake with Master John Bradford. As the two stood chained amongst the faggots, Master Bradford turned to him and said: "Be of good comfort, brother, for we shall have a merry supper with the Lord this night."

"And thus they both ended their mortal lives, without any alteration of their countenance, being void of all fear," hoping to obtain the prize of the fame they had long run at; to the which I beseech Almighty God happily to conduct us, through the merits of Jesus Christ our Lord and Saviour. Amen."

CHAPTER V

Joan Horns

ONE OF THE SMITHFIELD MARTYRS

KING HENRY VIII was dead, and his young son, Edward VI, had been proclaimed king, in January, 1547. People who were able to think over, and to weigh, the affairs of the kingdom at this crisis, were wondering whether the sweet, gentle-minded, delicate boy of ten would be able to wield the sceptre and hold the reins of government strongly enough to curb the ambitions of the nobles and ministers who surrounded him; and to rule wisely the harassed and disturbed people of his realm.

Only ten years of age. "Just the same age as we are, Margaret Ellis," said Joan Horns to her friend. "Yes, only a little boy. Right glad am I that it is Edward, and not Margaret Ellis to rule England," rejoined Margaret.

Joan smiled, in full agreement with this

sentiment. "It's safer to be plain and humble people who are nought to any-one," she observed. "We are not likely to become objects of vengeance or plot."

Poor JOAN HORNS! She was too young to know of the possibilities of those days, though whispers from time to time reached even Billericay, their native village, in Essex. There were rumours of court in-trigues; of the Princess Mary, next heir to the throne, an ardent Roman Catholic; of Princess Elizabeth, her step-sister, the king's favourite sister, and much discus-sion there would be about them.

Joan Horns and Margaret Ellis lived on happily in Billericay, enjoying each other's society as girl-friends do, and telling each other their troubles and joys.

Both the girls were seriously inclined, and regularly attended the services of the church. The use of the Latin language was now abolished entirely, and the ser-vices rendered in English, so they were able to understand. Then came a time when they became converted—trusting in the Lord Jesus alone for salvation.

But a dark hour dawned once more for England. The young king, who had been sinking for a long time, died in the summer of 1553. Lady Jane Grey was made queen, but in about nine days she was imprisoned. Mary, the dreaded heir to the throne, was proclaimed, and England was again in the hands of Roman Catholic rulers, and a long five years of cruel persecution was about to begin.

Of course Joan and Margaret would talk of all these happenings, and sometimes, with white faces and trembling lips would express fears as to whether they could remain steadfast should trial come their way. And already that trial seemed near.

"Heard you, Margaret, that all married clergy may have to leave their churches, and that the Latin Mass is to be restored."

"Yea, Elizabeth Thackvel of West Burstead hath so informed me. In Great Burstead, Sir John Mordaunt and Edmund Tyrrell have already received orders from Bishop Bonner to watch for those who keep to the ways of King Edward VI."

"May the Lord Who died for us give us

of His strength, " said Joan solemnly, laying her hand lovingly on her friend's shoulder.

"Faithful unto death may we be, " was Margaret's reply.

And so the time passed on until February of 1556. Sir John Mordaunt and Edmund Tyrrell, Esquire, Justices of the Peace in Essex, had been very busy, very vigilant. Sharp watch had been kept on one and another, and at last, after persecuting many for holding aloof from the Romish priests and the idolatrous mass, the victims were collected, to be sent to London, there to appear before the cruel Bonner.

There is a letter from Sir John Mordaunt and Edmund Tyrrell to Bishop Bonner, dated March 2nd, 1556, in which Margaret Ellis is named with several others, and also speaks of some "sent before. " This letter would be carried by those in charge of the prisoners and presented to Bonner when the party arrived in London.

So we see there came a day when Joan Horns, too, was called for by the priest, and a sheriff, and after a short period of imprisonment was taken on horseback to the great city. It is most probable that after this journey she and Margaret did not see anything of each other again until the day of Joan's entrance into Heaven, for the prisoners were tried separately, not all together.

Margaret Ellis, at her examination, was asked where she bore her candle on Candlemas Day—where she had received ashes on Ash Wednesday—where she was confessed—and where she had received the sacrament of the altar last Easter? To which questions she replied that "she had not borne a candle, nor received ashes, nor been confessed, as her conscience did not allow her to do those things." Candlemas was a festival in honour of the Virgin Mary, who is not to be worshipped—the receiving of ashes was a denial of the sufficiency of the Blood of Christ to redeem, for, in the dedicatory prayer it is declared: "Whosoever shall sprinkle themselves with these ashes for the redemption of their sins may obtain health of body and protection of soul." Margaret Ellis knew that the

Lord Jesus Christ had redeemed her. As to confession, she confessed to Christ only. And as to the sacrament, she had been to Much Burstead Church, to the English Communion. For these replies she was adjudged a heretic, and committed to Newgate Prison, to await her appointed hour of burning. But in prison she fell ill and died, and thus she reached her Heavenly Home sooner and by a quieter, less painful way, than did Joan Horns.

Joan Horns, Elizabeth Thackvel, and Katherine Hut had been sent up to London together, and the same questions were put to them as had been put to Margaret, and they, being all of the same mind, all answered alike bravely, though examined separately. And Joan Horns boldly announced that she forsook all the abominations of the Romish Church.

And thus these courageous young girls, so steadfast in refusing to worship the "consecrated wafer," which, they declared, was nothing but bread, and to worship it was idolatry; and so loyal to the Lord Jesus that they determined to suffer death rather than deny Him as the all-sufficient Saviour, were condemned to be burnt.

On the 16th of May, that sweet month of delicate flowers and tender green foliage, so full of hope—they "were led to Smithfield," the great burning-place in those terrible years, and there, cruelly bound to the stake, "gave their bodies to the tormentors: their spirits they commended to God, for whose glory they were willing and ready to suffer whatsoever the cruel hands of their enemies should work against them, dying more joyfully in the flaming fire, than some of them that burned them did, peradventure in their beds."

Yes, beyond the flames they could see Heaven opened, as Stephen did. They knew that a wonderful welcome awaited them when they reached their Homes— all pain and suffering forgotten at the first look into the face of the Lord Jesus:

"Where everlasting Spring abides,
And never withering flowers."

CHAPTER VI

Agapetus

MORE THAN CONQUEROR

A BOY of fifteen, clad in the *toga virilis* (which was his right as just passing from boyhood to youth), was climbing a hill in Italy. It was 23 miles from Rome, and faced the Alban hills. Behind him was the town of Præneste, a lovely spot in the Apennines—a very favourite resort of notable persons on account of its beautiful situation and bracing air.

The villa of the Emperor Hadrian was there, that Hadrian who built a wall from the Tyne to the Solway, in Britain. Marcus Aurelius, the philosopher emperor, loved Præneste; perhaps some of his "meditations" were written there. Horace the poet stayed there often.

May be this boy, Agapetus, thought of these great personages as he climbed, and paused to look back on the beautiful town. His thoughts may have roved to Britain as his eyes rested on the Emperor Hadrian's villa—Britain, where that emperor's mighty wall had been strengthened only a few years before by another emperor— Severus Septimus. It had been a difficult work. The wild Caledonians resented the building of this wall, it put a stop to their raids on the prosperous and cultivated land of Britannia, they had fought fiercely and long, and Severus, an old man for those days (actually only about 65), had died at York, A.D. 211, worn out.

Agapetus turned his back on Præneste and surveyed the distant Alban hills beyond which stood Rome, the ruling City of the world. His thoughts, then, would naturally be of the reigning emperor, Alexander Severus, for Rome was full of excitement over the great triumph accorded to Alexander.

Alexander was but a boy himself when he came to the throne—just seventeen— A.D. 222. His reign had been a peaceful one for many years. He had reformed a

THE MARTYRDOM OF BISHOP HOOPER   (Chapter I)

To face page 48

JOHN BRADFORD AND JOHN LEAF AT THE STAKE
(Chapter IV)

great many abuses, and offended a good many people in doing it, whilst benefiting others. Then came war with Artaxerxes, King of Persia, in which Alexander was victorious, and he had just celebrated a great triumph in Rome. Many had brought news to Præneste of the mighty procession and great rejoicing in the city.

To every Roman boy that word "triumph" would present a vivid picture. He would see the victor enter the city at the Gate of Triumph to make the long slow progress to the Temple of Jupiter at the Capitoline Hill, his splendid chariot drawn by gorgeously bedecked horses— the gloomy prisoners, some chained to his chariot—the treasures and spoils of war—the brilliantly clad soldiers—the crowds of people all in white, cheering and acclaiming the man in the chariot as he drove slowly along the road.

In Præneste it had been the one topic. But there was other news, too. It was that all people were forbidden on pain of death to become Christians. And Agapetus was a Christian, a loyal follower of the Lord

4

Jesus Christ. To him the word "triumph"
had a higher, more glorious meaning than
it had to the ordinary person. He had read
a portion of the Word of God which said:
"Having spoilt principalities and powers,
he made a show of them openly, *triumphing*
over them in it" (Col. 2. 15).

The Lord Jesus, of Whom this was
written, had died and risen again.   He
had *triumphed* over death, and Hades, and
Satan.   Agapetus need not fear these
vanquished foes any more than he would
fear the captives walking in the triumphal
procession of Alexander Severus.

But there was one person of whom
Agapetus felt afraid, and that person was
himself. Would he prove faithless? Would
he deny the Saviour when brought to trial?

Already he had been spoken to for his
negligence of the gods of the Romans. It
had been marked that he never threw
incense on the altar, or paused in worship
before any image, and for this, he knew,
he would some day be punished. He knew,
too, how dreadful the punishment would
be, for he had often been forced to witness

the torturing of those who believed in
Jesus and who refused to sacrifice to idols.

Could he remain true to his Lord and
Saviour? As he thought of it he felt afraid
of himself—fearful lest he should yield and
do that thing they asked—acknowledge
their gods by throwing a few grains of
incense on the altar, and blaspheme Christ
—*deny* his Lord.

As he walked slowly down the hill he
remembered other precious words he had
heard from those inspired writings trea-
sured amongst the Christians: "Blessed
be God Who always causeth us to *triumph*
in Christ" (2 Cor. 2. 19).

Had not hundreds of believers suffered
shame and agony, and *triumphed*, looking
up to Heaven where Jesus awaited them?
He had seen it.

Again he remembered the precious words,
"Who shall separate us from the love of
Christ? Shall tribulation, or distress, or
persecution, or famine, or peril, or sword?
. . . . Nay, in all these things we are more
than conquerors through Him that loved
us. For I am persuaded, that neither

death, nor life, nor angels, nor principalities, nor powers, nor things present, nor
things to come, nor height, nor depth, nor
any other creature, shall be able to separate us from the love of God, which is in
Christ Jesus our Lord" (Rom. 8. 35-39).
"'More than conquerors through Him that
loved us,'" repeated the boy.   He was
glad he had seen it—glad he had witnessed
this power which enabled believers to be
more than conquerors.   "And thus, O
Lord, may it be for me," he said, fear
vanishing, and a deep, holy joy filling
his heart.

A few days later he was arrested, and
his captors placed him before an altar,
and filling his hands with incense, bade
him throw it on the fire in the name of one
of their heathen deities, and to blaspheme
Christ.   "I cannot worship your idols,"
said he.

Finding they could not bend him to
their will, they brought whips and scourged
him.   Then, because he still remained true
to his Lord, they hung him up by his feet.
But not even then would he yield.   He

found as Paul did, that "the Lord stood by him and strengthened him."

His persecutors, angered beyond measure that such a lad dared to resist their importunities, once again ordered him to sacrifice. Once again he gently but firmly refused, and they poured hot water on him. As he lay helpless and half conscious, they consulted what should be done, and one suggested that he be given to the beasts. There was to be a great entertainment on the morrow—gladiators fighting—contests of the net and trident—and the killing of many Christians by wild beasts in the arena. Agapetus should afford some enjoyment for the hundreds of spectators who would be at the games.

Accordingly, on the morrow, the heavy iron gates swung open, and Agapetus, with his fellow-sufferers, entered the sanded space. As they did so there came the roar of hungry lions, and other gates were opened to let the savage creatures rush upon their victims. But Agapetus saw them not. His heart was so uplifted now that he seemed almost in the presence of

Christ. That vast sea of faces around and above him were not visible to his eyes. He saw only the face of Christ. And when the ferocious wild beasts leapt upon him, his spirit took its flight Heavenwards—more than conqueror—where a loving welcome was given him by Christ Himself.

CHAPTER VII

Agnes

THE YOUNG PATRICIAN

AGNES was born in Rome during the reign of Diocletian, about the year A.D. 294. Her parents were of noble birth, and Agnes, doubtless, lived in a beautiful home, resplendent with mosaic floors, marble pillars, and porticoes, and cooling fountains. There were slaves who waited about in attendance, ready at a sign of the hand to bring luscious fruits or wine, to pull down a shade to keep the sun out, or raise one to let it in.

There were slaves for every purpose. Those beautiful marble pillars and walls were polished by the slaves who had charge of them, till they shone like glass, and everywhere in the home of a high-born Roman was all that luxury and ease could desire.

Very likely Agnes' home was on the

Pincian Hill, and from the porticoes she would look across the Campus Martius, that vast space where the soldiers drilled and trained.   Perhaps the great aqueduct stretching across the Campagna was visible. White Temples reared their heads here and there amid the great box trees planted by Augustus many years before.   Below was the stir of the busy Forum.

But under all the stateliness, and luxury, and seeming ease of these wealthy Romans lurked evil and danger.   Agnes, young as she was, knew that no life was safe from the power and cruelty of the Emperor.   Envy and malice could easily find a way to bring ruin and death to the highest.   Was there nothing secure—was there no one in whom one could trust?

Even when Agnes was quite a child these thoughts laid hold of her, and when she heard one day the story of Jesus, the Son of God, the Saviour, Who had come to die for our sins—Who had risen again and ascended to Heaven, how joyfully her heart received Him!

Here was Someone more powerful than

the mightiest Cæsar—One Who had given His life to save *her*, Who had shed His Blood that *she* might be washed from sin, and made meet for the inheritance of the saints in light. He was preparing a Home for *her* in His Father's house above the strife and evil of this world, where she would dwell for ever with Him.

Happy Agnes! Happy the day when her young heart found its Refuge in the loving Saviour and gracious Lord. No matter what awaited her in the gilded, glittering world in which her lot was cast for the present, her future with Him, in the courts and bliss of Heaven was assured.

She trod the marble halls of her earthly home now with a lighter step; her eyes shone bright and clear with the inner joy, and, had she dared, she would have broken into one of the sweet hymns she was learning amongst the Christians. But in those days to say: "Jesus died for me: I am His," would mean torture and death for the boy or girl who said it. So, for a time, our little Agnes said nothing except to those who were like-minded.

The Christians had a curious way of finding each other out. You would see one person drawing (as we draw sometimes idly with the point of a stick), the outline of a fish. That sign meant: "JESUS, SON OF GOD, SAVIOUR." The letters of the word fish in Greek are the initial letters of that sentence, so when a fish was drawn by one person before another, if that person looking on was a Christian, he or she would understand, and draw a fish, too; and thus, without a word they knew each other for believers in the Lord Jesus Christ. After that, the newly discovered Christian would be taken to the meetings in the Catacombs, the only place where they could gather safely and undisturbed.

The Catacombs form a maze of underground passages just outside old Rome, and at night the Christians would steal away in twos and threes to one of the entrances and make their way lighted by torches, to the appointed place of meeting. There in the torchlight, they would pray, and listen to the reading of such part of God's Word as they had in those days, and sing hymns, without fear of being heard. If you ever go to Rome, be sure to see the Catacombs, for they are there still. You will see the names of Christians in the burying places, many of them martyrs.

The years went by, for the most part filled with cruelty towards the Christians, but this persecution revived their strength, and purity, and simplicity, which had failed much during a long period of peace many years before.

The Emperor Diocletian was incensed against them by Galerius, his son-in-law and co-emperor, and he issued edict after edict to compel the Christians to deny and dishonour their Lord. Through the streets of Nicomedia and Rome, and all great cities, public proclamation was made that *all*—men, women, and children—were to go to the temples of the gods and sacrifice. Some Christians, through fear of the persecution which would follow, did as they were bid, but Agnes, young as she was, boldly refused.

As time went on, Galerius, with two of the three Emperors, became more vigilant and vindictive, and Agnes was taken and tortured. Strengthened by Christ Himself, she stood firm, and at last was ordered to be beheaded.

The executioner came towards her, a naked sword in his hand, and she smiled at him. Poor tortured child, she felt she could smile, for she knew of the joy and glory which lay beyond death. Heaven was a real place to her, and she would be face to face with her Saviour.

So she said: "I am now glad and rejoice that thou art come! I will willingly receive unto my bosom the length of this sword. I shall surmount and escape all the darkness of this world. Receive, O Christ, my soul that seeks Thee!" Then she knelt down, and with one swift stroke it was all over. Those standing by could see only the poor severed body. She, the real Agnes, was radiantly happy in the presence of her Lord—seeing Him, speaking to Him. Happy ever after! Thus she triumphed by grace.

CHAPTER VIII

Brave Jamie Douglas

THE COVENANTER

BEFORE I tell you the story of JAMIE DOUGLAS, I must remind you a little about the noble Scottish Covenanters. The Solemn League and Covenant was a declaration or vow made by Scottish people, in the reign of Charles I, to guard the Church from idolatry, and to uphold the Bible as its only standard of belief. Those who meant to stand by this declaration were called Covenanters.

They, and their ministers, suffered cruel persecution, torture, and death at the hands of the king's men; they had to hold their meetings, or conventicles, as they were called, in secret places, and, as the Covenanting ministers had all been turned from their churches, they had to find refuge where they could—in caves, in secret rooms, on the moorland, and in the deep woods and glens.

Every Covenanter was always ready to help, and feed, and shelter the homeless fugitive ministers; but it was a dangerous thing to do, and they were often killed for doing it.

Nevertheless, they helped each other in all ways, and the boys and girls bore a brave part in the terrible happenings of this period of forty-five years—1643-1688 — when William, Prince of Orange, came to the throne.

Life was very solemn, very sad to these children. Mothers, fathers, brothers, sisters were often ruthlessly separated and scattered, or put to death. From day to day they never knew what terrible things might happen.

Now you will understand the story of Jamie Douglas and others of the children of the Covenant about whom I want to tell you. I expect some of you know how very delightful it is to run and jump about on the moor, and to see rabbits and other wild things scurrying here and there; to see butterflies hover over the bushes, and to hear bees humming about the gorse and heather. The sunshine all round, the fleecy clouds sailing across the blue of the sky; a lark mounting upwards, and singing its song of praise; and a hundred other things contributing to your pleasure as you tramp or skip and jump along.

Well, many years ago a little lad named Jamie Douglas was walking over a rocky, broken, heather-covered, rough Scottish moor. He was not buoyant and free in his walk; he did not whistle or sing, and his progress was a careful one for two reasons. One was that underneath his plaid he was carrying a parcel of food, and the other reason was because he wanted to reach his destination without being seen. So, very stealthily he went—past great bushes, now in the shadow of a great rock, now on an open space, into cover again.

Some little distance away, on the hill-side, overhung by sturdy ash and oak there was a cave, and in that cave was an old Scottish minister named Tam Roy. He was waiting for the arrival of Jamie

Douglas with the parcel of food from Jamie's mother.

Tam Roy was hiding from Claverhouse, that cruel man who was hunting for the brave Covenanters all over the moor, to put them to death.

So you understand why Jamie is trying so carefully to keep as much out of sight as possible. He *must* give Pastor Tam Roy the food, and he must *not* betray the old man's hiding place. Well, he knows that soldiers may be lurking near, but he hopes for the best, and he does his best.

On he goes, it is only a short distance now—this great rock with small rowan trees in its crevices is a place to wait and look around. No one in sight, but as he reaches the end of this rock and rounds the corner—there—waiting for him—are *soldiers*, some of Claverhouse's men.

Rough hands seized the little lad, and his plaid is nearly pulled off, displaying the parcel he carried. "Ha! lad! You are bearing this food to the old rebel, Tam Roy—are you not?" exclaimed one of his captors.

THE EXECUTION OF CHRISTIANS IN ROME
Dafrosa is seen kneeling, knowing that she will be the next martyr.
(Chapter IX)

ONE OF THE FAITHFUL PASTORS PREACHING TO THE COVENANTERS
Men on the hills are on the watch for their persecutors   (Chapter XI)

Jamie went very white, but he said nothing. The man could feel the boy's body trembling, and he laughed. "Come you before our leader," he said, pushing Jamie along in the direction of a cruel-looking man who was seated on a boulder.

The leader looked into Jamie's white, brave face, and asked: "Where is the old man hiding, boy?" "I will not tell you," was the answer. "Not if I let you go free?" Jamie's eyes flashed, and his reply was given in one word, *"No!"*

The man leapt up, infuriated, and gripping the boy's shoulder: "You dare defy me," he roared. "See here, what your end shall be if you refuse to tell me where that old man is."

He dragged the boy forward to the edge of a chasm close by. It was dark, and deep, and rugged with broken rocks. The trees clinging here and there to its steep sides seemed small and far away in those gloomy depths.

"Down there you'll go. There are hungry wolves about, and carrion crows to pick your bones clean." As he spoke,

5

the man seized Jamie and held him suspended over the gulf for a moment, then roughly set him down again.

"That's where you'll go," said he. "It's awfu' deep," the boy said, shudderingly, then he looked round on the men. "Would ye throw me down—hae ye nae bairns at hame?" he pleaded.

"Come, come," said the angry leader, fearful perhaps lest his intention be frustrated, "tell me, or I fling you down the chasm." "I canna tell—I canna tell," sobbed Jamie. Then he looked up at the sky. The Lord Jesus, he remembered, had stood up to receive Stephen. He would receive Jamie, too.

"Throw me doon. I wil'na show ye what ye want," he said.

Furious at the boy's steadfastness, the man seized the light form, and lifting him high, cast him far over the edge. But before his frail body reached the bottom of that deep crevasse, it is more than probable that his brave spirit had winged its flight heavenwards.

Pastor Tam Roy waited in his secret

cave in vain for Jamie's coming; and the mother went often to her cottage door to see if Jamie was returning. But when the quiet stars shone in the sky, and still he did not appear, she knew that her next meeting with Jamie would be in the Home above, that glorious place where evil will never come, but perfect safety, perfect peace, and perfect love will be ours for ever.

"And there, among the saved at last,
For ever blest and glad,
The mother dear, and old Tam Roy,
Shall meet their bonnie lad."

Chapter IX

Bibiana

FAITHFUL UNTO DEATH

BIBIANA was a young Roman girl, born about the time in which Constantine's three sons were reigning. These sons were named Constantine, Constantius, and Constans. Constans reigned over Italy and Africa. Bibiana, with her sister, Demetria, and her parents, lived in Rome, and Constans was their Emperor.

The Christian religion had been made the State religion by Constantine the Great (father of the three emperors) about A.D. 313, nearly 50 years before, and many Christians held high office instead of being hunted and tortured for their faith. I am sorry to say they were not so brave, and so loyal to their Lord as in the time of persecution. Many were very wealthy and thoroughly worldly.

But there was a great number who

remained true, and amongst them were
Flavian, the father of Bibiana and Demetria, and Dafrosa their mother. Flavian
held a good post under Government for
many years, and his was a happy Christian
household.

During the reign of Constans, and of
Constantius his successor, they were not
persecuted, but in the year 361 A.D., Julian
a nephew of Constantine the Great came
to the throne, and there were changes.
He declared himself a Pagan. He re-
nounced Christianity; he restored heathen
temples and statues, and did all he could
to bring in again the worship of heathen
gods.

He did not openly persecute the Christians, but ordered that they should be
treated coldly, and allowed his officers
to murder them, even conniving at their
murders, and the banishments brought
about by these cruel statesmen.

So it happened that one morning Bibiana
and Demetria found their parents very sad,
and on inquiring the cause the young girls
were told that the Governor of Rome,

Apronianus, had ordered their father into exile unless he would give up his faith. "And I cannot give up my faith in the Lord Who bought me. Rather exile than that, for some day we shall all reach that Home whence none can drive us."

"Oh, father," cried the delicate little Demetria, "cannot we go with you?" "The Governor will not permit it. He intends our separation, for he knows what pain it will give us." And so it proved. A few days afterwards came officers to this happy home, who tried again to persuade Flavian to turn pagan. On his firm refusal, the father was torn from his dear ones, and desolate indeed was the home without him.

Later came orders from the Governor that Dafrosa should be conveyed to prison on account of her faith, and thus the two girls were practically orphaned. The Governor was not content with this. First he gave command that the mother should be starved to death—and shortly after, being anxious to bring her death about quickly, ordered that she should be beheaded, and she was. Her husband died in exile, and the two girls, without any to protect them, were deprived of all their property, and brought before the Governor.

There, before that dread tribunal they stood, looking as though a breath would take them away, and more than one stony heart softened at the pathetic sight. Not so Apronianus. In loud tones he shouted at them that they must renounce their faith and acknowledge the Roman gods.

Bibiana looked at her frail little sister. Demetria looked at Bibiana, and her lips framed one word, "No." Bibiana took the cold little hand in hers, and turning to the Governor, said boldly: *"We will die rather than deny our Saviour.* Do what you will, we shall reach our Heavenly Home. You cannot take from us the treasure He has in store." "Say you so? And you, you fragile flower"—turning to Demetria and letting his cruel eyes rest on her face—"do you, too, prefer torture and death to throwing a few grains of incense on that altar there?" *"I will not dishonour Him Who died for me,"* Demetria answered bravely. She looked round in a dazed way, and gripping her sister's hand tightly, then, with a sigh, she sank to the ground. Bibiana raised her head, and laying her hand on Demetria's heart, found it was still. "Blessed be God, she is free!" she cried joyfully. "He has called her to Himself."

There was something of a stir at the girl's sudden death, but Apronianus soon recovered. He determined that anyhow this one remaining member of the family should yield. "See what your obstinacy has cost your sister," said he. "Surely you will obey me." "Sir," replied Bibiana, "long ago there lived two men who declared they ought to obey God rather than men. And I, God helping me, will stand firm, though I am but a maid."

"Sayst so? Then in a brief hour thou shalt be as she is," roared Apronianus.

"She is beyond your reach—she is at Home. And I will gladly bear all your malice to reach that shore," Bibiana said.

Can you picture the brave girl standing there before her judges? Apronianus in his gilded chair in front of her, separated only by a few feet—the rest of the Council ranged on either side of him—the soldiers in the background and round the walls. Every eye upon that slight figure, and watching the glory-light on her face as she steadfastly pronounces her refusal to sacrifice to their gods.

There was silence for a moment, then the Governor gave a short, sharp order. Bibiana was removed from the tribunal to be scourged to death. Did she think, before she lost consciousness under the cruel lashes, of Jesus, Who was scourged and spat upon, and crowned with thorns? He must have been near her, with a gracious, strengthening touch, as her body sank beneath the blows and she drew her last breath.

A rough, dark path to Heaven, was it not? But, ah, when she reached that shore!—

> "What radiancy of glory!
> What bliss beyond compare."

CHAPTER X

Andrew Hislop

A BOY OF THE COVENANT

IN October of 1684 the cruelly treated Cameron Covenant clan affixed a warning to the church door saying that they would punish anyone who continued to persecute them. They declared that they were forced to this by their enemies in self-defence.

This notice caused a great stir among the king's men, who had been chasing and killing the Covenanters, and a command was issued in the king's name that if any person gave shelter or food or help in any way to a Cameronian, that person would be severely treated.

One day, some weeks after the issue of this command, which the cruel Claverhouse was enforcing everywhere, a poor, ill-clad, sick man was slowly making his way to a cottage on the moor near to a hamlet.   It was a long and painful journey, for he could scarcely walk at all; he had to creep along, now sinking down behind a rock to rest awhile out of sight, then on again a short way.

As it became dusk, and the bleak hills behind him were being blotted out by the coming night, he crawled on more steadily, more continuously. At last he reached the door of a cottage. He could see the glow of a fire through the windows. He raised his hand and knocked feebly, for his last ounce of strength was almost gone; he was nearly losing consciousness.

Inside that little home the feeble knock caused consternation. The widowed mother looked at her two boys in alarm. Who could be visiting them at such an hour? Some of those terrible dragoons?

Bracing herself, she rose to open the door, but the elder of her sons, a lad of seventeen, Andrew Hislop, quickly put out his arm to stay her.

"I will see who it is, mother," said he, and before she could prevent it, he was unbarring the door.

There, in the dim light he saw a figure lying on the flagstones, the hands falling across the threshold as the door opened.

Andrew stooped over the fallen man, guessing at once that some despairing fugitive was seeking a refuge. The mother gave but one keen glance: "Bring him in, Andrew. It is one of the proscribed Cameronians."

The lad obeyed, and in a short time the wanderer was lying in bed, conscious enough to express his thanks to the widow and her son, and to assure them he would not burden them long.

The days went by, and each hour the stranger's end drew nearer. He was glad of this, he told them, for the suffering and sickness away in the cold hills had been terrible. And in that place whither his feet were tending, he said with a smile, "the wicked cease from troubling and the weary are at rest."

"Aye," replied the good woman, in a trembling voice, "'twill be a bonnie greetin' ower yonder. Nae waefu' weepin' there!"

Then he spoke very sorrowfully of the dangerous position in which she had placed herself and her boys by giving shelter.

"We'll be verra carfu', " was her answer. "An' come what may, I couldna dae less. "

He smiled at that, and replied that if a cup of cold water given in the Name of Christ should receive a reward, how much greater would be their recompense, who had ventured their lives. She would see, when accounts were made up in yon bright Home.

Andrew Hislop stood by listening to this conversation, and his heart glowed at the thoughts it called forth.

Then came a day when the spirit was set free, and, in accord with the stranger's wish, they buried the poor, worn-out body in a field nearby, after nightfall. Very quickly and very quietly did they dig the grave, and after covering the remains, made the ground around and above appear as undisturbed as possible.

But it was discovered a few days later. A Dragoon came knocking at the widow's cottage, and searching questions were asked. She could not hide the fact that she had sheltered the dying Cameronian and buried the body in the spot where the prying eyes of the soldiers had found it. "Ye know full well that punishment will be meted out to you for this," said the man roughly.

"Aye, I know," she answered. And before nightfall she and her sons were walking homeless on the hills. Her cottage had been pulled down, and all her possessions had been destroyed or confiscated.

History does not tell us how they managed to live as they wandered from one place to another, seeking a home and work. No doubt there were many who fed and helped them, but Mrs. Hislop would be unwilling to bring anyone into trouble for befriending her and her boys. So they moved about, staying nowhere long enough to endanger those who were kind to them.

Then came a terrible day. They were not far from Eskdale. "See, mother!" cried the younger boy. "Soldiers! And see yon handsome man!"

There was no time to hide. The regiment swept down the road. The "handsome man," John Graham, of Claverhouse, the persecutor, drew up in front of the trio. It was upon Andrew that those cruel eyes rested; and it was for Andrew those scowling brows grew blacker. Here was the insolent lad who, aided by his mother, had sheltered a rebel!

A few sharp commands, and Andrew is a prisoner. The poor mother and her younger boy watched the soldiers disappearing round the bend, Andrew in the midst.

They were taking him to Eskdale, to be brought before Sir James Johnstone, of Westerhall, a man who once was a Covenanter, but was now their greatest enemy.

Sir James Johnstone was overjoyed to see Claverhouse and his youthful prisoner. There was no need to have a trial—Andrew was guilty, and should be shot at once, said the Laird of Westerhall.

But Claverhouse, who only about ten days before, had ordered the brutal shooting of John Brown of Priesthill, seemed unwilling that Andrew should be killed.

The Laird of Westerhall, however, urged him, almost commanded him, and so Claverhouse gave the order. Three dragoons lined up, shoulder to shoulder. Andrew was told to cover his eyes with his bonnet. He would not do so, but stood upright and fearless, and raised his Bible aloft. "I can look you in the face," said he. "I have done nothing to be ashamed of. But you, when you shall come to be judged by what is written in this Book, how will you look in that day?"

Three shots rang out, and the boy fell dead. They buried his body among the sweet heather and fern of Craighaugh, but his spirit had long ere that reached the heavenly shore, and been received into Glory.

Chapter XI

Isabel and Marion

THE CAMERONIANS

TIMES of persecution in Scotland which the Covenanters passed through were a trial to all, even boys and girls were called upon to suffer a great deal.

Claverhouse and his men were always ready to frighten them. Claverhouse himself would collect the girls and boys of country hamlets, some as young as six years, and placing them in front of his dragoons, ordered the children to pray, as he meant to kill them. In order to alarm them he sometimes ordered the soldiers to fire over the heads of the little things. He then would say he would spare them if they would tell him where their fathers and big brothers were hiding.

But the little children, generally, were not told about the hiding places of their elders, and could not say. Even if, as in some cases they did know, they would not tell.

Growing up as they did, surrounded by persecutors and swift death—hearing of the terrible fights in the hamlets and on the moors—finding that fathers or big brothers never returned—it was natural that the children of the Covenant were grave and thoughtful beyond their years. It seems as if they could never have known what childhood was—certainly not the gay childhood we know nowadays. Death seemed ever near. But, ah! some of these children could see a long way into Heaven by faith.

There were two girls, named ISABEL ALISON and MARION HARVIE, about 17 years old; both of them Cameronians— that clan which was to be hunted down, and none of which was to have shelter or help.

These two girls, because they were Covenanters, were seized and imprisoned in Edinburgh. Whilst they were there their judges sent a minister, named Archibald Riddell, to visit them.

Once he had been a minister of the Covenant, but the prospect of persecution had been too much for him. He had given way, and was preaching against the Covenant. He was not of those steadfast bands who gathered on the high and lonely moor at Irongray, 1678, to celebrate together for the last time the Lord's Supper. Many of that gathering were killed afterwards. It is more than likely that Isabel and Marion had been there.

The two girls regarded this man very solemnly whilst he tried to persuade them to conform as he himself had done. And when he ended they assured him it was useless.

He looked at them in silence for a moment or two. Was he thinking, with some regret, of his weakness as compared with the steadfastness of these frail lasses?

"Shall we pray?" he asked them. But the girls refused.

"Your prayers will be like unto your discourse," said Marion. "We could not join you in such a prayer."

"I will not mention your principles, but

only ask the Lord to let you see the evil of your doing," he answered.

"We are not evil doers, nor busybodies. We do but stand by the truths of the Bible and the Lord Jesus Christ. How, then, can we join you in that prayer?" was the answer of both, given almost in one breath.

And so Archibald Riddell left them. He saw that they could not be moved. They would stand by the Covenant whatever betide.

As he turned at the door for one last look at the young girls he must have realised how different *he* was. They were facing death for conscience' sake—he had stifled his conscience, and was taking the ease which his conformity afforded. But was he as happy as those two persecuted, imprisoned maidens? No, he knew he was not. He had weakly denied his Lord by turning to the idolatrous form of worship which was enjoined by the king, and enforced by Claverhouse and his soldiers. Better far for him had he yielded up his life like the brave and gallant Hugh Mackail, the young Covenant minister,

who died on the scaffold, crying out joy-
ously: "Welcome, sweet Lord Jesus. Welcome eternal life. Welcome Glory!"

Riddell's last glance at the bright girlish
faces must have cut him to the heart, and
filled it with regret and remorse. He
would never forget them and their courageous stand for the Lord. It is most likely
that it gave him strength in the sufferings
which later he endured at the hands of the
king's men.

Next day Marion and Isabel were brought
again before their judges in Edinburgh
Council Hall. Word of their refusal to
listen to Archibald Riddell in prayer had
been passed on to the court officials, and
the hard-hearted Bishop Paterson taunted
them with it.

"Marion," said he, "you did own ye
never would hear a curate. I warrant ye
shall be forced to!"

He ordered one of his curates to pray.

The curates who had been foisted on the
people were rough and rude—picked up
from anywhere, and they enjoyed the
power they held. You may be sure that

this curate's prayer would have been more of a coarse sermon preached at the girls, than a prayer to the Heavenly Father in the Name of the Lord Jesus Christ.

Marion knew this. She *had* heard curates years before. She also knew that false representations would be made, if they consented to listen to this "please all." "Come Isabel, dear friend, let us sing our beloved Twenty-Third Psalm," she cried.

At once Isabel joined her, for all the Covenant children learnt those sweet words as soon as they could talk.

> "The Lord Himself my Shepherd is:
> He makes me down to lie
> In pastures green; He leadeth me
> The quiet waters by."

Clearly and sweetly they sang it through, and especially that verse about the valley of the shadow of death, for they themselves would soon be passing through that valley. But His rod and His staff would comfort them, they knew, and they would dwell in the House of the Lord for ever. The curate's prayer was not heard at all.

They were led to the Grassmarket on

January 26th, 1681, to be beheaded. The crowd watched the girls on the scaffold, where mocking words and jeers followed them. The young martyrs did not mind. Isabel said she had hoped for such a lot, but had never thought it would be such a high one. And Marion cried out to the Lord—so near, so beautiful did He seem— "O, my Fair One, My Lovely One, come away!"

Just before the executioner struck off their heads, they sang the 84th Psalm. Read it, and you will see how happy, how sure, they felt. They could see where they were going:

> "Far o'er yon horizon rise the City towers,
> Where our God abideth; that Fair Home is ours."

As you read this true testimony, ask yourself, had you been in their position, how would you have acted? The Lord Jesus is the only One who could enable you.

CHAPTER XII

Rasalama

THE FIRST OF THE MADAGASCAR MARTYRS

MADAGASCAR is that big island which lies on the east of Africa, about 250 miles from the coast. It is 900 miles long, 300 broad—twice the size of Britain.

It is a wonderful island, with beautiful scenery, and full of useful things. There rosewood grows, that wood of which dinner tables are made, and cabinets. Mahogany trees are abundant—you may have a mahogany sideboard in your home. Then ebony is another familiar wood from Madagascar; and when you do raffia work, as so many boys and girls do, you can think of raffia palms in Madagascar. Rice pudding should remind you of the same place, for there are green fields of rice there.

The British paid their first friendly visit there in 1816, during the reign of a good king, Radama I. Of course the people were idolaters, and very dreadful things happened in this beautiful island.

The London Missionary Society sent missionaries over in 1818, and were encouraged by Radama. In ten years' time (1828) there were 30,000 people who could read, and the language had never been written before 1823.

During the reign of good King Radama I, the teaching and preaching of the Gospel went on rapidly, but when he died, in 1827, a wicked queen, Ranavalona, one of his wives, succeeded, after having cleared the way to the throne by killing the rightful heirs.

She was an idolater, and soon put a stop to the missionaries' work. They knew this would happen, so they hurried to get a number of New Testaments and Bibles printed in the Malagasy language before the queen sent out her order for all missionaries to leave the country.

They managed to finish 70 Bibles, and during the persecution which the Christians suffered all through Ranavalona's reign, which lasted about 30 years—she

was crowned, June, 1829; died, July 16,
1857—those who had Bibles used to put
them into boxes, bake them in the oven,
or bury them in the ground. At times
they were dug up and read by stealth.

One of these native Christians wrote to
a missionary: "It is thought that we shall
forget the Word of God as we have no
teachers now. The queen does not understand that the best teacher is with us still,
the Holy Spirit."

She thought she could stamp out Christianity, with no missionaries there, and, as
she imagined, no Bibles; but her own son,
Prince Rakoto, was a Christian, and she
loved him so much that she allowed him to
have his way. He protected the Christians
whenever he could, and often saved them
from death by warning them.

There was a brave young Christian girl
of high degree called Rasalama. When she
was standing in her own house one morning
she heard the steady tramp of men coming
towards it—officers from the queen!

One of them bore a long spear made of
silver, with the queen's name engraven

on it. This spear was a very important and well-known thing in Madagascar. When it was brought to a house it was fixed in the door by the officer, and no one might pass in or out of that house.

Rasalama knew all this. She knew that she was to be imprisoned for being a Christian, but she was not afraid; rather she rejoiced to suffer for the Name of Christ. Very shortly after the arrival of the silver spear she was taken to the town prison where other Christians were.

The prison officers wanted to find out the names of every one who met for prayer and Bible reading. After trying several Christians, they came to Rasalama, and told her that they already knew the names, so it was no good her refusing to tell. Poor deceived Rasalama then spoke of seven of her friends, thinking that they were already arrested. They were not, but the information enabled the officers to find them.

Rasalama was very, very sad over that. She spoke about it to the other prisoners, and said she could not understand why people who behaved so well and so quietly, who never stole, and never spoke ill of any, should be condemned to perpetual slavery, for that was what Ranavalona expected.

This was overheard by an officer, and Rasalama, who was singing hymns nearly always, was put into irons and beaten. For days she was chained in a position which caused her great pain, but she did not mind. She was thinking of that time when she would reach Heaven.

At last they carried her away, on August 14th, 1837, and as they went she was singing and saying how joyful she was that she had heard and obeyed the Gospel.

On the way they passed the place where she had often attended, and she cried: "Oh there—there I heard the words of the Saviour!" A mile farther they came to a kind of dry moat, from which the distant hills could be seen all round, and green fields of rice, and peaceful villages. The moat itself was the place where criminals were always killed, and their bones were still lying there. But Rasalama's eyes of faith were looking at the Land that is very far off, and the Saviour ready to receive her.

The executioners gave her permission to pray, so she knelt on the dried grass and prayed, as Stephen, the very first martyr, did: "Lord Jesus, into Thy hands I commit *my spirit.*" Then she was slain by the executioners' cruel spears, and her wounded body fell to the ground. What would the bystanders have said if they could have seen her happy spirit on its Homeward flight. Even the heathen executioners said: "There is some charm in this Christian religion which takes the fear of death away." Yes—for God has said He will ransom them from the power of the grave; and we can say, "O Death, where is thy sting? O Grave, where is thy victory"? (1 Cor. 15. 55). Jesus has conquered death. And this was how Rasalama, the first martyr of Madagascar, glorified the Lord Jesus Christ. Are you ready to meet the Lord?